Your Mother's Heart
333 Questions to Ask Your Mom Before She Dies to Cherish Her Forever

Your Mother's Heart
333 Questions to Ask Your Mom Before She Dies to Cherish Her Forever

Celebrate Her Life, Capture Her Wisdom, and
Strengthen Your Bond Through Meaningful
Conversations and Questions

Aria Capri Publishing Group
Devon Abbruzzese & Mauricio Vasquez
Toronto, Canada

Authors:
Aria Capri Publishing
Devon Abbruzzese
Mauricio Vasquez

First Printing: September 2024

ISBN- 978-1-998402-74-8 (Paperback)
ISBN- 978-1-998402-75-5 (Hardcover)
ISBN- 978-1-998402-76-2 (Electronic)

Your Mother's Name:

_____

_____

TABLE OF CONTENTS

INTRODUCTION

A mother's heart holds a lifetime of stories, wisdom, and experiences that shape who she is. These stories—of love, sacrifice, resilience, and joy—are the threads that connect us to her journey. They influence how we see ourselves, how we view the world, and how we relate to one another. Yet, in the busyness of life, we often let these precious stories remain untold, missing the opportunity to truly understand the woman behind the role of "mother".

This book is designed as a bridge between you and your mother, offering thoughtful questions that open up meaningful conversations. It's more than just a collection of prompts; it's an invitation to explore the rich narrative that has shaped her life. Each question is crafted to reveal the depth of her experiences, from the dreams she's chased and the challenges she's overcome, to the values that have guided her along the way.

Engaging in these conversations is not just about learning her past—it's about creating a dialogue that will strengthen your bond and preserve the essence of her legacy for generations to come. These discussions will give you a window into her world, illuminating the choices, beliefs, and moments that have defined her journey. Whether it's how she navigated motherhood, her reflections on love and family, or the joys and sorrows that shaped her, you'll come away with a deeper understanding of her heart.

In today's fast-paced, digital world, taking the time to pause and connect with your mother in a meaningful way is a gift—both for you and for her. This book serves as a reminder that the stories we share, the wisdom we exchange, and the memories we create together form the foundation of our family's history. As you ask these questions, listen closely to her answers, for they hold the keys to not only understanding her life, but also illuminating your own.

Let these pages guide you toward rediscovering the richness of your mother's story, fostering a deeper connection, and ensuring that her legacy lives on in your heart and the hearts of future generations.

A JOURNEY AT YOUR OWN PACE: SAVORING EVERY CONVERSATION

This book is meant to be a gentle companion, offering you the freedom to engage with its questions in a way that feels natural and enjoyable. There is no set timeline or specific approach to follow—this is a journey that you and your mother can embark on at your own pace, without any pressure or urgency. Whether it's during a quiet morning together, a cozy afternoon at home, or an evening spent reminiscing, these questions are designed to spark meaningful conversations when the moment feels right.

You may choose to ask a single question each day, allowing your mother's answers to unfold slowly and thoughtfully, creating a space for deeper understanding and reflection. Or perhaps you'll explore several questions in one sitting, letting the conversation flow naturally, as you move from one cherished memory to the next. There is no right or wrong way to use this book—only the opportunity to uncover the wisdom, experiences, and stories that have shaped your mother's life.

The beauty of this book lies in its flexibility. Some days, a single question may open the door to an emotional and enriching conversation that lingers for hours; other times, the response might be brief, but still filled with meaning. The intention isn't to rush through these questions, but to savor the journey, enjoying the connection and the stories that emerge along the way.

By allowing these conversations to unfold at their own pace, you create a space where your mother can share her stories without feeling rushed or overwhelmed. This book is a guide, not a checklist—a way to slowly and thoughtfully explore the legacy she has built throughout her life. Whether it's one question a day or several over the course of a week, the goal is to enjoy the time spent together, appreciating the stories that bind you and ensuring that her memories are never lost.

So, take your time. There is no hurry—only the joy of discovering, connecting, and cherishing the moments and memories that will stay with you forever.

SHARE YOUR STORY: HELP OTHERS CONNECT

As you journey through these pages and uncover the stories that have shaped your mother, I hope this book has brought you closer to her and deepened your connection in meaningful ways.

Your thoughts and reflections are invaluable, not only to me but to future readers who, like you, seek to preserve the essence of their mother's legacy. If this book has touched your heart or sparked cherished conversations, I would be grateful if you could share your experience by leaving a review.

Your words have the power to inspire others to embark on their own journey of discovery, ensuring that more mothers can create lasting memories through these heartfelt questions. Thank you for being a part of this legacy.

To share your review, simply scan the QR code provided— your feedback means the world to me.

CHAPTER 1

Childhood and Family History

Uncover the foundational stories, traditions, and early memories that shaped your mother's identity, revealing the roots that have influenced her journey through life.

1. Can you describe the home and neighborhood where you grew up? What was the atmosphere like, and how did it influence your childhood?

2. What are some of your earliest and most vivid memories from childhood? Why do you think these moments stand out to you?

3. How did your parents (or caregivers) shape your sense of identity and values, and what lessons from them have stayed with you throughout life?

4. What role did family traditions play in your upbringing, and are there any specific customs or rituals that hold special meaning for you?

_____

_____

_____

_____

5. Can you share a favorite story or memory about one of your siblings or close relatives, and how that relationship shaped your childhood?

_____

_____

_____

_____

6. What were some of the challenges you faced as a child, and how did you navigate them? What support systems or coping mechanisms helped you during those times?

_____

_____

_____

_____

7. How did the cultural or societal expectations of your childhood influence your choices and aspirations as you grew older?

_____

_____

_____

_____

8. What role did religion, spirituality, or philosophy play in your family life, and how did those beliefs influence your upbringing?

_____

_____

_____

_____

9. What hobbies, activities, or pastimes did you enjoy as a child, and how did they shape your interests as you grew older?

_____

_____

_____

10. Can you share a memory of a time when you felt particularly proud or accomplished as a child, and what that moment meant to you?

11. What was your relationship with your grandparents like, and how did their presence or absence influence your childhood and family dynamics?

12. Were there any significant world events or societal changes that impacted your family life or your perspective as a child?

13.Looking back, what do you believe were the most important lessons you learned from your childhood that have continued to guide you through life?

CHAPTER 2
Life Transitions and Milestones

Explore the pivotal moments of change—such as adulthood, marriage, and retirement—that defined your mother's paths, shaping who she became and how she views success.

1. Can you describe a key moment when you felt you had fully transitioned into adulthood, and how did it change your perspective on life?

2. What was one of the most significant milestones in your life, and how did it shape who you are today?

3. How did your view of success evolve as you moved through different life stages, and what experiences influenced that evolution?

4. What was one of the most challenging transitions you faced, and what helped you navigate through that period of change?

_____

_____

_____

_____

5. Can you share your experience of marriage or partnership, and how that relationship contributed to the person you are today?

_____

_____

_____

_____

6. How did you approach major life decisions, such as choosing a career, starting a family, or deciding when to retire, and what factors guided you?

_____

_____

_____

_____

7. Can you describe a time when you had to reinvent yourself or start a new chapter in life, and what that experience taught you about resilience?

8. What was the transition to motherhood like for you, and how did it change the way you saw yourself and your role in the family?

9. How did your career evolve over the years, and what were the key moments or decisions that defined your professional journey?

10. What did retirement or the idea of stepping back from work mean to you, and how did you prepare for that transition?

_____

_____

_____

11. What was one of the biggest risks you took in life, and how did that decision shape the direction your life took afterward?

_____

_____

_____

12. How did you balance the changes in your own life while supporting the transitions or milestones in the lives of your loved ones?

_____

_____

_____

13. Looking back, what life transition or milestone do you believe had the most profound impact on who you are today, and why?

_____

_____

_____

_____

CHAPTER 3

Health and Well-Being

Delve into your mother's experiences with physical and mental health, discovering how she navigated challenges and sustained her well-being throughout her life.

1. What habits or practices have you prioritized throughout your life to maintain your physical health, and how have they changed over time?

_____

_____

_____

2.Can you share a time when you faced a significant health challenge, and how you managed to cope both physically and emotionally?

_____

_____

_____

3.What role has mental health played in your life, and what practices have helped you maintain a sense of balance and peace?

_____

_____

_____

_____

4. How did you balance the demands of family, work, and self-care, and what advice would you give to others about finding time for themselves?

_____

_____

_____

_____

5. What lifestyle changes have you made over the years to improve your well-being, and what prompted those changes?

_____

_____

_____

_____

6. How did you approach physical fitness throughout your life, and what activities or routines brought you the most joy or benefit?

_____

_____

_____

_____

7. Can you share a story about a time when you felt overwhelmed, and how you managed to restore your mental or emotional well-being?

_____

_____

_____

_____

8. What role did nutrition play in your approach to health, and how did your understanding of food and well-being change over the years?

_____

_____

_____

_____

9. What advice would you give about handling the natural aging process and maintaining well-being as you get older?

_____

_____

_____

_____

10. How did your emotional well-being affect your physical health, and what have you learned about the connection between mind and body?

_____

_____

_____

_____

11. Can you describe a time when you had to advocate for your own health, and what did you learn from that experience?

_____

_____

_____

_____

12. How have relationships with family or friends influenced your overall sense of well-being, and what role did social support play in your health?

_____

_____

_____

_____

13 . Looking back, what do you believe is the most important lesson you've learned about taking care of your health, both physically and mentally?

_____

_____

_____

_____

CHAPTER 4
Values, Ethics, and Beliefs

Understand the guiding principles and moral compass that have steered your mother's decisions, providing insight into the beliefs that have shaped her worldview.

1. What core values have guided your decisions throughout life, and how did you develop these beliefs?

2. Can you share a story where your values were tested, and how you remained true to what you believe in?

3. How did your upbringing or early experiences influence your sense of right and wrong?

4. Have your values or beliefs changed over time? If so, what experiences led to those changes?

_____

_____

_____

_____

5. What role has spirituality, religion, or philosophy played in shaping your values and guiding your actions?

_____

_____

_____

_____

6. Can you describe a time when you had to make a difficult decision based on your principles, even if it wasn't the easiest path?

_____

_____

_____

_____

7. What ethical values have been most important to you in raising children, and why did you prioritize these particular values?

_____

_____

_____

_____

8. How do you approach disagreements with people whose values or beliefs differ from yours, and what have you learned from those interactions?

_____

_____

_____

_____

9. What role has honesty played in your life, and how have you managed situations where the truth was difficult to face or share?

_____

_____

_____

_____

10. Can you share a moment when compassion or empathy led you to make a decision you might not have otherwise made?

_____

_____

_____

11. How have you balanced standing up for what you believe in with maintaining harmony in relationships, especially during disagreements?

_____

_____

_____

12. What lessons about integrity and doing the right thing do you hope to pass on to future generations?

_____

_____

_____

13. Looking back, what do you believe is the most important principle or value that has guided your life, and how has it shaped the person you are today?

_____

_____

_____

CHAPTER 5
Love, Relationships, and Family Dynamics

Examine the bonds and connections that defined your mother's life, from romantic relationships to family ties, revealing how she built and maintained meaningful relationships.

1. Can you share the story of how you met my father (or your partner), and what drew you to each other in the early days of your relationship?

_____

_____

_____

2. What values or principles were most important to you when building a strong relationship with your partner, and how did you nurture that connection over time?

_____

_____

_____

3. How did you and your partner handle disagreements or conflicts, and what advice would you give about resolving issues while keeping a relationship strong?

_____

_____

_____

4. What role did family traditions or cultural values play in shaping your approach to love, marriage, or partnerships?

_____

_____

_____

5. How did your relationships with your siblings or other close family members impact your understanding of family dynamics and love?

_____

_____

_____

6. What lessons about love and relationships did you learn from your parents, and how did those lessons influence the way you built your own family?

_____

_____

_____

7. Can you share a story about a time when you faced a challenge in a relationship, and how you and your partner (or family) overcame it together?

_____

_____

_____

_____

8. How did you balance your role as a partner with your role as a mother, and what challenges or rewards did you experience in doing so?

_____

_____

_____

_____

9. What is one of the most meaningful gestures of love or support you've experienced in your life, and how did it impact your relationships?

_____

_____

_____

10. How have your friendships contributed to your sense of love and connection, and what role have friends played in supporting your family life?

_____

_____

_____

_____

11. What advice would you give about maintaining close family ties, especially through periods of change or distance?

_____

_____

_____

12. How did becoming a parent change your perspective on love, and how did it affect the way you approached other relationships in your life?

_____

_____

_____

13. Looking back, what do you believe is the most important lesson you've learned about love and family, and how do you hope to pass that lesson on to future generations?

_____

_____

_____

_____

CHAPTER 6
Parenting and Legacy

Reflect on your mother's experiences raising children and the legacy she hopes to leave behind, capturing the values and wisdom she wishes to pass to future generations.

1. What was one of the most rewarding moments you experienced as a parent, and how did it shape the way you viewed motherhood?

2. What values or lessons did you consider most important to teach your children, and how did you go about instilling those values in us?

3. Can you share a story about a particularly challenging time in your parenting journey, and how you overcame that challenge?

4. How did becoming a mother change your understanding of legacy, and what do you hope your legacy will be in terms of the values and lessons you leave behind?

_____

_____

_____

_____

5. How did you balance your own personal dreams and goals with the demands of raising a family, and what advice would you give about finding that balance?

_____

_____

_____

_____

6. What were some of the most important traditions or rituals you introduced to our family, and why were they meaningful to you?

_____

_____

_____

_____

7. Can you share a lesson you learned from your own parents about raising children, and how did that lesson influence your parenting approach?

_____

_____

_____

_____

8. How did you handle moments when you didn't have all the answers as a parent, and what did you learn from those experiences?

_____

_____

_____

_____

9. What hopes did you have for your children as they grew older, and how did those hopes influence the way you guided us?

_____

_____

_____

_____

10. What do you believe are the key ingredients to raising a close-knit, loving family, and how did you work to foster that environment?

_____

_____

_____

11. What role did forgiveness, understanding, or patience play in your approach to parenting, and how did you model those traits for us?

_____

_____

_____

12. How have your views on parenting evolved as your children have grown older, and what new perspectives have you gained from watching us become adults?

_____

_____

_____

13. Looking back, what do you hope will be the most important lesson or value that your children and future generations carry forward from your example?

_____

_____

_____

_____

CHAPTER 7
Personal Growth and Lifelong Learning

Discover how your mother continued to evolve, learn, and adapt, embracing new experiences and personal growth in her life.

1. What was one of the most significant learning experiences of your life, and how did it change your perspective or direction?

2. How have your goals or ambitions changed over the years, and what motivated those shifts in your personal growth?

3. What new skills or hobbies have you embraced as an adult, and what inspired you to pursue them?

4.Can you share a time when you had to step outside of your comfort zone, and how that experience contributed to your personal growth?

_____

_____

_____

_____

5. How did you approach learning new things while balancing the demands of work, family, and personal life?

_____

_____

_____

_____

6. What books, people, or life experiences have had the greatest influence on your personal development, and why?

_____

_____

_____

_____

7. Can you describe a moment when you realized that you had changed or grown in a significant way? What brought about that change?

_____

_____

_____

_____

8. What challenges did you face in maintaining a growth mindset throughout your life, and how did you overcome moments of self-doubt or stagnation?

_____

_____

_____

_____

9. How have your relationships—whether with family, friends, or colleagues—contributed to your ongoing learning and personal growth?

_____

_____

_____

_____

10. What life lesson took you the longest to learn, and how did finally understanding it affect your personal growth?

_____

_____

_____

11. What do you believe is the key to staying open to new experiences and continuing to grow, even in later stages of life?

_____

_____

_____

12. Can you share a story about a time when you taught someone else an important lesson, and what that experience taught you about yourself?

_____

_____

_____

13. Looking back, what do you believe are the most important principles or habits that have helped you continue growing and evolving throughout your life?

_____

_____

_____

CHAPTER 8
Career and Professional Life

Trace the journey of your mother's professional life, uncovering the decisions, challenges, and achievements that defined her career and work–life balance.

1. What inspired you to pursue the career path you chose, and how did your early experiences shape your professional goals?

---

2. Can you share a story about a pivotal moment in your career that significantly shaped your professional direction?

---

3. What was one of the biggest challenges you faced in your career, and how did you overcome it?

---

4. How did you balance work with family life, and what advice would you give about maintaining that balance?

_____

_____

_____

_____

5. What accomplishments in your career are you most proud of, and why do they hold special meaning to you?

_____

_____

_____

_____

6. Can you describe a time when you had to take a professional risk, and what did you learn from that experience?

_____

_____

_____

_____

7. What role did mentorship or collaboration play in your professional growth, and how did these relationships influence your success?

_____

_____

_____

_____

8. How did you handle setbacks or failures in your career, and what did those experiences teach you about resilience and success?

_____

_____

_____

9. What was one of the most rewarding aspects of your career, and how did it align with your personal values?

_____

_____

_____

_____

10. Can you share a moment in your career when you felt truly challenged, and how did you push through to achieve success?

_____

_____

_____

11. How did your professional life evolve over time, and what key decisions or moments led to those changes?

_____

_____

_____

12. How did you approach networking and building professional relationships, and what advice would you give about creating strong connections in a career?

_____

_____

_____

13. Looking back, what do you believe is the most important lesson you've learned from your career, and how has it shaped the person you are today?

_____

_____

_____

_____

CHAPTER 9
Social and Cultural Reflections

Explore how societal changes and cultural shifts have influenced your mother's perspectives, shaping her views on the world and her place within it.

1. What major societal or cultural shifts do you feel had the most impact on your life, and how did they shape your views on the world?

2. How have your views on gender roles and expectations evolved over time, and what experiences shaped those changes?

3. Can you share a story about a time when cultural norms or societal expectations influenced a major decision in your life?

4. How did growing up during a specific era or political climate affect your perspective on social justice or equality?

_____

_____

_____

_____

5. What cultural values or traditions from your upbringing have you maintained, and which ones have you chosen to leave behind or adapt?

_____

_____

_____

_____

6. How did significant global events, such as wars, political movements, or economic changes, affect your sense of security or your approach to life?

_____

_____

_____

_____

7. How have technological advancements, such as the rise of the internet and social media, changed the way you interact with the world, and how do you view these changes?

---

8. What role did cultural diversity and exposure to different perspectives play in shaping your understanding of the world?

---

9. Can you share a time when you felt out of step with societal norms or expectations, and how did you navigate that experience?

10. How has your view of social activism or advocacy changed over time, and what role do you think individuals should play in shaping society?

_____

_____

_____

11. What cultural or social issues have you become more passionate about over the years, and what events or experiences led to that passion?

_____

_____

_____

12. How do you think future generations will view the cultural and societal changes you've witnessed, and what lessons do you hope they learn from your experiences?

_____

_____

_____

13. Looking back, how do you believe societal progress or setbacks have influenced your overall philosophy on life and your place in the world?

_____

_____

_____

_____

CHAPTER 10
Dreams, Aspirations, and Regrets

Delve into the dreams your mother pursued—or left unfulfilled—and the reflections and regrets that have shaped her outlook on life.

1. What were some of your biggest dreams or aspirations when you were younger, and how did they shape the choices you made in life?

_____

_____

_____

2. Can you share a dream or goal that you accomplished, and what that achievement meant to you?

_____

_____

_____

3. Were there any dreams or aspirations you had to set aside, and how did you feel about making that decision?

_____

_____

_____

_____

4. How did your dreams and aspirations evolve as you grew older, and what life experiences influenced those changes?

_____

_____

_____

_____

5. Can you describe a time when you took a big risk to pursue a dream, and what did you learn from that experience?

_____

_____

_____

_____

6. What was one of your proudest moments, and how did it compare to the dream you originally had?

_____

_____

_____

_____

7. Are there any dreams you still hope to pursue, and what do you believe is stopping you from going after them now?

8. Looking back, is there anything you regret not doing, and how has that shaped your perspective on life or future decisions?

9. . How did your role as a mother influence the way you pursued your dreams, and were there any dreams that were fulfilled through your experiences raising children?

10. Can you share a story about a time when you overcame a significant challenge in pursuit of a dream, and how did that shape your perspective on persistence?

---

11. What advice would you give to someone who feels like they've missed out on achieving their dreams, and how can they find fulfillment later in life?

---

12. Is there a dream or aspiration you had as a child or young adult that still resonates with you today, and why do you think it has endured?

---

13. Looking back, do you believe you lived a life true to your dreams and aspirations? If not, what would you do differently, and how has that shaped the legacy you want to leave?

CHAPTER 11
Challenges and Resilience

Uncover the adversities your mother faced and the resilience she built, learning how she overcame obstacles and emerged stronger.

1. Can you share a story about one of the toughest challenges you've faced in life, and how you found the strength to overcome it?

2. What role did your personal values or beliefs play in helping you stay resilient during difficult times?

3. How did you navigate moments of self-doubt or fear when faced with adversity, and what helped you push through?

4. Can you describe a situation where things didn't go as planned, and how you adapted to those unexpected changes?

_____

_____

_____

_____

5. What was one of the hardest decisions you've ever had to make, and how did you find the courage to make it?

_____

_____

_____

_____

6. Can you share a moment when you felt overwhelmed, and how you managed to regain control and move forward?

_____

_____

_____

_____

7. What life lesson did you learn from overcoming a major setback, and how did it change the way you approached challenges afterward?

_____

_____

_____

_____

8. How have relationships—whether with family, friends, or colleagues—helped you remain resilient during challenging times?

_____

_____

_____

_____

9. What was a time when you had to rely on hope or faith to get through a difficult experience, and how did that influence your outlook on life?

_____

_____

_____

_____

10. How did you balance personal resilience with caring for others during a difficult period, especially when your loved ones were also struggling?

11. Can you share an example of a challenge that seemed insurmountable at the time but that you now look back on with pride?

12. What practices or habits have you developed over the years to help you stay grounded and resilient when life gets tough?

13. Looking back, what do you believe was the most important quality that helped you remain resilient throughout your life, and how do you hope to pass that lesson on to future generations?

CHAPTER 12
Advice and Wisdom

Capture the life lessons and practical advice your mother has gathered, offering timeless guidance for navigating life's complexities.

1. What is the most important piece of advice you've ever received, and how has it shaped the way you live your life?

_____

_____

_____

2. What life lesson took you the longest to learn, and why do you think it was such a challenge to fully understand?

_____

_____

_____

3. If you could give one piece of advice to your younger self, what would it be, and why do you think it's important now?

_____

_____

_____

_____

4. What advice would you give about handling life's inevitable challenges or setbacks, and how did you develop that mindset?

_____

_____

_____

_____

5. What have you learned about building and maintaining strong relationships, and what advice would you give about fostering meaningful connections?

_____

_____

_____

_____

6. How did you learn to manage stress and find balance in your life, especially when juggling multiple responsibilities?

_____

_____

_____

_____

7. What advice would you give about following one's passion or pursuing dreams, and how have your own experiences shaped that advice?

_____

_____

_____

_____

8. What do you believe is the key to living a fulfilling and meaningful life, and how have you worked toward that fulfillment?

_____

_____

_____

_____

9. How did you develop a sense of confidence in yourself, and what advice would you give to someone struggling with self-doubt?

_____

_____

_____

_____

10. What financial advice have you found most valuable, and how has managing money played a role in shaping your life decisions?

_____

_____

_____

_____

11. What do you believe are the most important qualities to cultivate in order to lead a life of integrity and purpose?

_____

_____

_____

_____

12. How did you develop resilience in the face of hardship, and what advice would you give to someone going through a difficult time?

_____

_____

_____

_____

13. Looking back, what do you believe is the most valuable lesson you've learned in life, and how do you hope future generations will benefit from it?

_____

_____

_____

_____

CHAPTER 13
Hobbies, Interests, and Passions

Explore the hobbies and passions that brought joy and fulfillment to your mother's life, revealing the activities that enriched her everyday experiences.

1. What hobbies or interests have you been most passionate about throughout your life, and how did you first discover them?

_____

_____

_____

2. Can you share a memory of a time when you felt fully immersed in a hobby or passion, and what did that experience mean to you?

_____

_____

_____

3. How have your hobbies or passions changed over time, and what influenced those shifts?

_____

_____

_____

4. How did you make time for your hobbies or personal interests while balancing other responsibilities like family and work?

5. What role have your hobbies played in maintaining your well-being or providing stress relief throughout your life?

6. Were there any hobbies or passions you wished you had more time to pursue, and how do you feel about those missed opportunities?

7. How did your interests or hobbies connect you with others, and did they help you build meaningful relationships or communities?

_____

_____

_____

_____

8. Can you share a skill or hobby you were proud of mastering, and what did you learn from that journey of growth?

_____

_____

_____

_____

9. What hobbies or interests have brought you the most joy as you've grown older, and why do you think those particular activities have endured?

_____

_____

_____

_____

10. Did any of your hobbies or passions influence your career or professional life, and if so, how did they shape your path?

_____

_____

_____

11. How did you encourage your children or others to explore their own hobbies and interests, and what advice would you give about following one's passions?

_____

_____

_____

12. Can you describe a time when you shared one of your hobbies or interests with a family member, and how did that experience strengthen your relationship?

_____

_____

_____

13. Looking back, what do you believe is the most valuable lesson you've learned from pursuing your hobbies or passions, and how has it shaped your life?

_____

_____

_____

CHAPTER 14
Technology and Modern Life

Investigate how your mother adapted to technological advancements and societal changes, reflecting on how these innovations shaped her life.

1. Can you remember the first major technological advancement you experienced, and how did it change your daily life?

---

2. How did you adapt to the rise of the internet and digital communication, and what impact did it have on your personal and professional life?

---

3. What technological change in your lifetime do you believe has had the most profound impact on society, and why?

---

4. How have advancements in technology influenced the way you raised your children, and how did you balance technology use in family life?

_____

_____

_____

_____

5. Can you share a memory of a time when you had to learn to use a new technology, and how did you feel about embracing it?

_____

_____

_____

_____

6. What role does technology play in your life today, and how do you feel about the way it has integrated into everyday activities?

_____

_____

_____

_____

7. How has social media changed the way you connect with friends, family, or the world, and what are the positives and negatives you've experienced?

_____

_____

_____

_____

8. What differences do you see in how people communicate today compared to when you were younger, and how has technology influenced that change?

_____

_____

_____

_____

9. How have you seen technology change the way we work, and what challenges or opportunities has it created in your own professional life?

_____

_____

_____

10. Can you share a time when technological innovation made a significant difference in your life, perhaps in terms of convenience, access, or opportunity?

11. How do you feel about the pace at which technology is advancing, and do you ever feel overwhelmed by trying to keep up with it?

12. What advice would you give to future generations about managing the balance between technology and human connection?

13. Looking back, what do you think are the most important lessons you've learned from adapting to modern technology, and how has it shaped your view of the world?

CHAPTER 15
Generational Comparisons

Contrast your mother's experiences with those of today, exploring the differences and similarities between her generation and yours.

1. What do you think are the biggest differences between your generation and mine, particularly in terms of how we approach life's challenges?

2. How do you think growing up in your time compared to growing up today, and what do you believe were the advantages and challenges of each?

3. What do you think are the biggest similarities between your generation and mine, and how do you see those common values or experiences continuing through future generations?

4. How was family life or parenting different in your generation compared to today, and what do you think is better or harder now?

_____

_____

_____

_____

5. What role did technology play in your life growing up, and how does that compare to how technology influences people's lives today?

_____

_____

_____

_____

6. What was the biggest societal or cultural change you witnessed growing up, and how does it compare to the changes happening in the world today?

_____

_____

_____

_____

7. How do you think attitudes toward work and career have changed between your generation and mine, and what do you think are the pros and cons of these shifts?

8. What advice do you think your generation would give to mine about handling life's responsibilities, and what advice do you think younger generations could offer in return?

9. How did societal expectations around gender roles or identity differ in your generation, and how do you feel about the changes happening today?

10. What values or traditions from your generation do you hope will continue, and what changes do you think are necessary for future generations?

11. How has the pace of life and communication changed between your generation and today's, and how do you feel about the impact of these changes on relationships and community?

12. How do you think your generation approached issues like mental health or emotional well-being compared to today, and what lessons could each generation learn from the other?

13. What do you believe was easier or more fulfilling about life in your generation, and what aspects of today's world do you think offer more opportunities or advantages?

CHAPTER 16
Legacy and Impact on Others

Reflect on how your mother believes she has impacted others, from mentoring and community involvement to the relationships she has nurtured.

1. How do you believe you've made an impact on the lives of others, whether through family, work, or your community?

_____

_____

_____

2. Can you share a time when you mentored or helped guide someone, and what did that experience teach you about leadership and support?

_____

_____

_____

3. What values or lessons do you hope your children, grandchildren, or others will carry forward as part of your legacy?

_____

_____

_____

4. How have your relationships, whether with family, friends, or colleagues, shaped the legacy you believe you're leaving behind?

_____

_____

_____

_____

5. What impact do you think your community involvement or volunteer work has had, and how has that shaped your sense of purpose?

_____

_____

_____

_____

6. What do you believe is the most important way to leave a positive mark on others, and how have you strived to do that throughout your life?

_____

_____

_____

_____

7. Can you share a moment when someone expressed how you impacted their life, and how did that feedback shape your view of your own legacy?

_____

_____

_____

_____

8. How have you balanced pursuing your own goals with helping others along the way, and what have you learned from that balance?

_____

_____

_____

_____

9. What role has kindness or empathy played in your interactions with others, and how do you believe these traits have contributed to your legacy?

_____

_____

_____

_____

10. In what ways do you think your career or professional contributions have impacted those around you, and what aspect of that impact are you most proud of?

_____

11. How do you hope your actions or life choices have inspired others, whether family members or people outside of your immediate circle?

12. What do you think is the most important lesson about life and legacy that you want to pass down to future generations?

13. Looking back, what aspect of your life's work or relationships do you believe will have the longest-lasting impact, and why?

CHAPTER 17
Cultural Identity and Heritage

Examine the cultural heritage and traditions that influenced your mother's identities, revealing how her roots shaped her sense of self.

1. What aspects of your cultural heritage have had the biggest influence on shaping who you are, and how did they impact your sense of identity?

2. Can you share a family tradition or custom that was particularly meaningful to you growing up, and why did it hold such importance?

3. How did your parents or grandparents pass down cultural values or traditions, and how did these shape your understanding of your roots?

4. How did cultural norms or expectations in your family affect the choices you made in life, such as education, career, or relationships?

_____

_____

_____

_____

5. Were there any cultural traditions or values that you chose not to carry forward, and what prompted that decision?

_____

_____

_____

_____

6. What was it like growing up in a family that practiced certain cultural or religious traditions, and how did it shape your worldview?

_____

_____

_____

_____

7. How did your cultural identity change as you interacted with people from different backgrounds or as you lived in different places?

_____

_____

_____

_____

8. What role does language play in your cultural heritage, and how did speaking or learning that language affect your connection to your roots?

_____

_____

_____

9. Can you share a story about a time when you felt particularly connected to your cultural heritage, and how did that experience impact you?

_____

_____

_____

_____

10. What cultural foods, music, or celebrations were a central part of your upbringing, and how do they still hold significance for you today?

_____

_____

_____

11. How did your family's cultural background influence the way you approached parenting, and what values or traditions did you hope to pass on to your children?

_____

_____

_____

12. Were there any challenges or tensions you faced balancing your cultural identity with other societal influences or personal beliefs?

_____

_____

_____

13. Looking back, what do you believe is the most important aspect of your cultural heritage that has shaped your sense of self, and how do you hope future generations will embrace that legacy?

_____

_____

_____

CHAPTER 18
Spiritual Journey and Reflections

Delve into your mother's spiritual beliefs and journeys, exploring how her faith and existential reflections have evolved over time.

1. What were the earliest influences on your spiritual beliefs, and how did they shape your understanding of faith or spirituality?

2. Can you share a time in your life when your spiritual beliefs were challenged, and how did you navigate that experience?

3. How have your spiritual or religious beliefs evolved throughout different stages of your life, and what prompted those changes?

4. What role has prayer, meditation, or other spiritual practices played in your daily life, and how have they impacted your overall well-being?

_____

_____

_____

_____

5. Was there a specific event or moment when you felt particularly connected to a higher power or a greater sense of purpose?

_____

_____

_____

_____

6. How has your understanding of life's meaning or purpose changed as your spiritual beliefs have evolved?

_____

_____

_____

_____

7. How have you balanced your spiritual beliefs with the practical challenges of everyday life, such as work, family, or hardship?

_____

_____

_____

_____

8. In times of difficulty, what role has faith or spirituality played in helping you stay resilient or find hope?

_____

_____

_____

_____

9. How did your spiritual beliefs influence your approach to parenting or raising a family, and what values did you hope to pass on to your children?

_____

_____

_____

_____

10. What do you think is the most important spiritual lesson you've learned in your life, and how has it influenced your worldview?

_____

_____

_____

11. Have your spiritual beliefs changed the way you think about life after death or the nature of the soul? If so, how?

_____

_____

_____

12. How do you find spiritual connection or inspiration in everyday life, and how does that guide the way you live?

_____

_____

_____

13. What wisdom from your spiritual journey would you most like to pass down to future generations, and why do you think it's important?

_____

_____

_____

_____

CHAPTER 19
Social Relationships and Networking

Explore the friendships and social circles that enriched your mother's life, offering insight into her broader support systems and social dynamics.

1. Can you share a story about one of your most meaningful friendships and how that relationship impacted your life?

2. What qualities did you value most in the friendships you've built over the years, and how did those friendships help shape who you are?

3. How have your social circles evolved throughout different stages of your life, and what influenced those changes?

4. What role did community and social networks play in supporting you during challenging times, and how did those relationships help you overcome adversity?

---

5. How did you maintain close relationships with friends and family members while balancing the demands of work, family, and other responsibilities?

---

6. What are some of the most important lessons you've learned from the friendships you've had, and how did those lessons influence the way you relate to others?

---

7. Can you share a time when a friendship or social connection surprised you by becoming more meaningful than you initially expected?

_____

_____

_____

_____

8. How did you navigate conflicts or misunderstandings in your friendships, and what did those experiences teach you about communication and trust?

_____

_____

_____

_____

9. What role did social or community gatherings, such as clubs, religious groups, or events, play in building your social network?

_____

_____

_____

_____

10. How have friendships with people from different backgrounds or cultures influenced your perspective on life and relationships?

_____

_____

_____

11. What do you believe is the key to maintaining lifelong friendships, and how did you stay connected to those who were most important to you?

_____

_____

_____

12. Can you share a time when you acted as a mentor or source of support for someone in your social circle, and how did that experience impact you?

_____

_____

_____

13. Looking back, what do you believe was the most important aspect of your social relationships, and how have they enriched your life over the years?

_____

_____

_____

_____

CHAPTER 20
Financial Life and Economic Lessons

Trace your mother's financial decisions and economic experiences, uncovering the lessons she has learned about managing money and navigating financial challenges.

1. Can you share a memory of an early financial decision you had to make, and how did it shape your understanding of managing money?

_____

_____

_____

2. What were some of the most important financial principles you learned from your parents or family growing up, and how did they influence your approach to money?

_____

_____

_____

3. How did you manage your finances during difficult economic times, and what strategies helped you stay resilient?

_____

_____

_____

4. What role did budgeting play in your financial life, and how did you learn to balance saving and spending?

_____

_____

_____

_____

5. How did you prioritize financial goals, such as buying a home, saving for children's education, or retirement, and what challenges did you face in reaching those goals?

_____

_____

_____

_____

6. What is one of the biggest financial mistakes you've made, and what did you learn from that experience?

_____

_____

_____

_____

7. How did you approach teaching your children about money, and what lessons or habits did you hope to pass on to us?

_____

_____

_____

_____

8. What advice would you give about managing debt, whether it's credit cards, mortgages, or loans, and how did you navigate those challenges in your own life?

_____

_____

_____

_____

9. What has been your philosophy about saving versus spending, and how did that philosophy evolve as your financial circumstances changed?

_____

_____

_____

_____

10. How did you prepare for major life transitions, such as marriage, having children, or retirement, from a financial perspective?

_____

11. What investments or financial decisions are you most proud of, and why did those choices stand out as particularly successful?

12. Looking back, how do you think gender roles or societal expectations influenced your financial decision-making, and what advice would you offer to others about navigating those dynamics?

13. What do you believe is the most important lesson about money that you've learned in your life, and how has that shaped the way you view financial success?

CHAPTER 21
Adventure, Travel, and Exploration

Discover the adventures and travels that broadened your mother's horizons, capturing the spirit of exploration and discovery in her life.

1. Can you share a memorable travel experience that had a profound impact on you, and how did it change the way you view the world?

_____

_____

_____

2. What was the first major trip you took, and how did it influence your love for adventure and exploration?

_____

_____

_____

3. Were there any trips or adventures that pushed you outside of your comfort zone? How did you grow from those experiences?

_____

_____

_____

_____

4. How did your experiences traveling to different places influence your understanding of other cultures, and what did you learn from those interactions?

_____

_____

_____

_____

5. What role did spontaneity play in your adventures, and can you share a story about a time when an unplanned event led to an unforgettable experience?

_____

_____

_____

_____

6. What was one of the most breathtaking or awe-inspiring natural places you've ever visited, and how did being there affect you emotionally or spiritually?

_____

_____

_____

_____

7. Were there any travels or adventures that changed your perspective on life, and if so, how did they shape your outlook?

_____

_____

_____

_____

8. How did your experiences with travel and adventure influence the way you raised your children or the values you tried to impart?

_____

_____

_____

_____

9. What is a place you've always dreamed of visiting but haven't yet been to, and why does it hold such significance for you?

_____

_____

_____

_____

10. Can you share a story about a travel companion who made an adventure more meaningful or memorable, and what did you learn from that relationship?

_____

_____

_____

11. What role did curiosity or a sense of wonder play in shaping your travel experiences, and how did you maintain that spirit of discovery over the years?

_____

_____

_____

12. How did you balance the desire for adventure with the responsibilities of family, work, or daily life?

_____

_____

_____

13. Looking back on all your travels, what do you believe was the most important life lesson you learned from your adventures, and how has it shaped who you are today?

_____

_____

_____

CHAPTER 22
Creativity, Art, and Expression

Explore your mother's engagement with the arts and creative pursuits, revealing how she expressed herself and found personal fulfillment through creativity.

1. What role has creativity played in your life, and when did you first realize that expressing yourself through art or other creative activities was important to you?

2. Can you share a particular project, piece of art, or creative endeavor that you are especially proud of, and why does it hold such significance for you?

3. How did creativity help you navigate difficult times, and what forms of expression gave you the most comfort or sense of release?

4. What creative activities or hobbies did you engage in as a child or young adult, and how did they shape the way you viewed the world?

_____

_____

_____

_____

5. How has your relationship with art or creativity evolved over time, and what has been the most significant shift in how you express yourself creatively?

_____

_____

_____

_____

6. Were there any artists, writers, musicians, or creative people who inspired you deeply, and how did their work influence your own creative journey?

_____

_____

_____

_____

7. How did you balance creative pursuits with other responsibilities, such as family, work, or personal commitments?

_____

_____

_____

_____

8. In what ways have you used creativity to connect with others, and how did those creative collaborations or exchanges enrich your relationships?

_____

_____

_____

_____

9. Was there ever a time when you faced creative block or lost your passion for artistic expression? How did you overcome that, or how did it change your relationship with creativity?

_____

_____

_____

_____

10. What role does creativity play in your day-to-day life now, and how do you continue to nurture your creative spirit as you get older?

11. How did your engagement with art or creativity influence the way you raised your children, and what creative values or activities did you hope to pass down to us

12. Can you share a moment when you realized that creative expression gave you a sense of fulfillment or purpose that was different from other parts of your life?

13. Looking back, what do you believe is the most important lesson you've learned from engaging in creative pursuits, and how has it shaped who you are today?

CHAPTER 23
Resilience and Coping Mechanisms

Dive into the specific strategies your mother used to cope with life's challenges, understanding how she maintained mental and emotional strength.

1. Can you share a difficult time in your life when you had to rely on inner strength and resilience to get through it, and what did you learn from that experience?

_____

_____

_____

2. What coping mechanisms have helped you manage stress or anxiety throughout your life, and how did you develop those strategies?

_____

_____

_____

3. When you felt overwhelmed by life's demands or difficulties, what did you do to find balance and regain a sense of control?

_____

_____

_____

4. What role did your support network—family, friends, or community—play in helping you through tough times, and how did those relationships strengthen your resilience?

_____

_____

_____

_____

5. Can you share a time when you felt uncertain or lost, and how you found the courage or strength to keep moving forward?

_____

_____

_____

_____

6. How have your resilience and coping mechanisms changed as you've grown older, and what life experiences contributed to that evolution?

_____

_____

_____

_____

7. When faced with personal setbacks or failures, how did you bounce back, and what did you learn about yourself through those experiences?

8. What role did spirituality, faith, or personal belief systems play in helping you cope with life's challenges, and how did they shape your resilience?

9. Were there any creative outlets, hobbies, or forms of expression that helped you cope with difficult emotions, and how did those activities support your well-being?

10. What advice would you give to someone going through a difficult time about building resilience and maintaining hope in the face of adversity?

_____

_____

_____

11. Can you recall a situation where you had to help someone else through a difficult time, and how did that experience influence your own coping mechanisms?

_____

_____

_____

12. How did you balance caring for others, such as family or friends, while still maintaining your own mental and emotional well-being?

_____

_____

_____

13. Looking back, what do you think is the most important lesson you've learned about resilience, and how has it shaped your view of life's challenges?

_____

_____

_____

_____

CHAPTER 24
Cross-Generational Wisdom

Capture the advice and wisdom your mother wishes to impart to future generations, ensuring her life lessons continue to guide and inspire.

1. What is the most important piece of advice you'd like to pass down to future generations, and why do you believe it holds such significance?

2. Can you share a story from your life that you believe illustrates an important life lesson or principle you want your children and grandchildren to remember?

3. What values do you hope future generations will continue to uphold, and how have those values shaped your own decisions and actions throughout life?

4. If you could give one piece of advice to your younger self, what would it be, and how do you think that advice would have changed your life?

5. What is the most important lesson you learned from your parents or grandparents, and how has that wisdom influenced the way you live your life?

6. How do you believe the challenges faced by your generation differ from those faced by today's younger generations, and what advice would you offer to help them navigate these new challenges?

7. What do you believe is the key to building meaningful relationships, and how have your experiences shaped your understanding of love, friendship, and family?

_____

_____

_____

_____

8. How do you define success, and how has your definition of success evolved throughout your life? What advice would you give about finding personal fulfillment?

_____

_____

_____

_____

9. What is one mistake or regret that you learned from, and how do you hope future generations will learn from it as well?

_____

_____

_____

10. What role do you think resilience and adaptability play in facing life's challenges, and how have you demonstrated these traits throughout your life?

11. What advice would you give about balancing ambition and contentment, and how did you find the right balance between pursuing your goals and appreciating what you have?

12. What traditions, family stories, or cultural practices do you hope will continue to be passed down through the generations, and why are they important to you?

13. Looking back, what do you believe is the most important legacy you hope to leave behind, and how do you want to be remembered by future generations?

CHAPTER 25
Daily Life and Simple Pleasures

Appreciate the simple pleasures and daily routines that brought contentment to your mother, revealing the joy found in everyday life.

1. What are some of the simple, everyday rituals or routines that brought you joy or comfort, and how did they become a meaningful part of your life?

2.Can you describe a typical day in your life during a particularly happy period, and what little moments or activities made that time special for you?

3.What are some of the small, seemingly ordinary things in life that you've come to appreciate most over the years, and why do they hold such significance for you?

4. How did you make time for yourself amidst the busyness of life, and what simple activities helped you relax and recharge?

_____

_____

_____

_____

5.. What role did food, cooking, or sharing meals play in your daily life, and how did those moments bring you a sense of satisfaction or connection?

_____

_____

_____

_____

6. Was there a particular time of day—morning, afternoon, or evening—that you looked forward to most, and what made it feel special to you?

_____

_____

_____

_____

7. HHow did spending time in nature—whether a walk, gardening, or simply sitting outdoors—contribute to your sense of happiness or tranquility?

8. What role did music, books, or other forms of art and entertainment play in your everyday life, and how did they help you unwind or find joy?

9. How did your morning routine set the tone for your day, and were there any small practices or habits that made mornings feel especially meaningful for you?

10. Can you share a memory of a time when the simple pleasures of life—whether a cup of coffee, a quiet moment, or a favorite hobby—brought you a deep sense of

happiness?

_____

_____

_____

11. How did you find joy in the everyday tasks and responsibilities of life, and what mindset or perspective helped you appreciate the routine moments?

_____

_____

_____

12. What were the small moments of connection with family or friends that made your daily life more meaningful, and how did those interactions bring you happiness?

_____

_____

_____

13.Looking back, what do you think was the most important lesson you learned about finding joy in everyday life, and how has it shaped the way you live?

_____

_____

_____

CHAPTER 26
Conflict Resolution and Difficult Conversations

Understand how your mother handled conflicts and tough discussions, exploring her approach to resolving disputes and navigating difficult conversations.

1. Can you share a time when you had to navigate a particularly difficult conversation, and what approach helped you reach a resolution?

2. What were the most important values or principles that guided you when resolving conflicts, whether with family, friends, or at work?

3. How did you handle disagreements or arguments within the family, and what techniques did you use to ensure everyone felt heard and understood?

4. Can you recall a time when a conflict didn't go as you hoped, and how did you handle the disappointment or frustration that followed?

_____

_____

_____

_____

5. What do you think is the key to approaching difficult conversations with empathy, and how did you balance your perspective with that of others?

_____

_____

_____

_____

6. Was there a time when you had to confront someone about something uncomfortable, and how did you prepare yourself emotionally for that conversation?

_____

_____

_____

_____

7. How did you handle conflicts in the workplace, and what strategies did you use to maintain professionalism while addressing disagreements?

8. Can you describe a time when you had to mediate a conflict between others, and how did you help both sides come to an understanding?

9. How did you find the balance between standing up for yourself and finding compromise in situations where you and someone else strongly disagreed?

10. What advice would you give about managing emotions—such as anger, frustration, or sadness—during difficult conversations?

_____

_____

_____

11. How did your approach to conflict resolution change over time, and what experiences led you to adjust the way you handled disputes?

_____

_____

_____

12. Was there ever a situation where you chose to walk away from a conflict rather than engage, and what did you learn from making that decision?

_____

_____

_____

13. Looking back, what do you believe is the most important lesson you've learned about resolving conflicts, and how has that shaped your relationships?

_____

_____

_____

_____

SHARE YOUR STORY: HELP OTHERS CONNECT

As you journey through these pages and uncover the stories that have shaped your mother, I hope this book has brought you closer to her and deepened your connection in meaningful ways.

Your thoughts and reflections are invaluable, not only to me but to future readers who, like you, seek to preserve the essence of their mother's legacy. If this book has touched your heart or sparked cherished conversations, I would be grateful if you could share your experience by leaving a review.

Your words have the power to inspire others to embark on their own journey of discovery, ensuring that more mothers can create lasting memories through these heartfelt questions. Thank you for being a part of this legacy.

To share your review, simply scan the QR code provided—your feedback means the world to me.

www.ingramcontent.com/pod-product-compliance
Lightning Source LLC
Chambersburg PA
CBHW031433120626
46545CB00006B/2386